NOTTINGHRE

Gⴑ

Prepare to be .y tales from
 .ire

Compiled by
Camilla Zajac

BRADWELL
BOOKS

Published by Bradwell Books
Carrwood Road, Chesterfield, S41 9QB
Email: info@bradwellbooks.co.uk

British Library Cataloguing in Publication Data: a catalogue
record for this book is available from the British Library.
1st Edition

ISBN: 9781910551905

Compiled by: Camilla Zajac
Design & Typesetting by: JenksDesign
Photograph Credits: iStock, Picture the Past,
Lee Haywood and Creative Commons
Print: CPI Group (UK) Ltd, Croydon, CR0 4YY

CONTENTS

Introduction   5

Creepy Castles   7

City Centre Spectres   13

Haunted Halls   21

Military Ghouls   30

Pub Phantoms   35

Haunted Churches, Abbeys and Priories   46

Towns with Ghostly Tales   59

Eerie Villages   68

Weird Woods   74

www.picturethepast.org.uk

'Picture the Past' is a not-for-profit project that started in 2002. We aim to make historic images from the library and museum collections across the whole of Derby, Derbyshire, Nottingham and Nottinghamshire, available to all via a completely free-to-use website. By early 2013 the 100,000th photograph had been added. The website also includes postcards, engravings and paintings and shows how life has changed in the region over the last few hundred years giving a fascinating insight into the work and lives of the people who lived there.

You can visit the website for free at www.picturethepast.org.uk

INTRODUCTION

You don't have to travel far in Nottinghamshire to hear a good ghost story about the county. Whether it's the spectral sightings at the National Justice Museum, the long-standing reports of the ghosts of Bestwood Lodge or odd tales of the Trip to Jerusalem, reputedly England's oldest pub, Nottinghamshire is home to many kinds of phantom visitors, if the stories are to be believed. Nottingham itself is said to be the fourth most haunted place in the UK.

But what is it that gives the city and county such a rich history of hauntings? Perhaps one reason is geography. Nottinghamshire's sandstone caves feature in a handful of the stories, suggesting that location and geology can play a part in the ghostly history of a place.

Some of these stories clearly have their roots in history, serving as a kind of alternative narrative to capture the events that shaped the area, like the tales of Nottingham Castle and Newstead Abbey. Whether or not you believe in ghosts you can see how the stories help to maintain a connection with events long gone, such as the tragic murder of Bessie Shepherd. But what of the weirder ones, like that of the little green men seen by a group of children at Wollaton Park or the ghost nurse encountered by other nurses at the Queen's Medical Centre Hospital? It's also interesting to note that, while some of these stories are clearly very old, others have their basis on sightings reported in the national or even international press within the last few years.

Whatever the reality behind these stories, they are important to the history and identity of Nottinghamshire. From the weird sightings in the city centre to the ghostly visitors in the towns and villages of the county, they help maintain our fragile connection with the past. They remind us of the fears, tragedies and dramas that affected the lives of ordinary people, just as they do today. A good ghost story changes the way we see a place, enriching our sense of its history. Perhaps ghost stories also serve as a kind of warning to tell us to take care, like the eerie tales of George's Hill in the village of Calverton. Whatever your view of ghosts, whether you're a cynic or an explorer of the paranormal, these stories of Nottinghamshire's otherworldly visitors should unnerve and intrigue.

CREEPY CASTLES

Nottingham Castle is not your typical castle. While it has a dramatic setting on the large promontory known as the Castle Rock, the building you see today is actually a Georgian mansion with just the gatehouse showing its medieval roots. Yet despite its comparatively modern appearance, Nottingham Castle is said to be home to two ghostly presences, closely connected by a struggle for power.

It all started in 1327, when Edward II was murdered by his wife, Queen Isabella and her lover, Roger Mortimer, Earl of March. While they then stated that Edward's son was king, they didn't let him have any real power, keeping that for themselves. In 1330, young Edward decided it was time to do something about this. But it wasn't going to be easy. As you would imagine for someone who enjoyed having power, Mortimer made sure that he was well protected, keeping a group of armed Welsh mercenary soldiers by him at all times, as well as sleeping in a locked room! But Edward was determined to succeed and, with some help and the clever use of the maze of tunnels which run beneath the castle, he managed to break into Mortimer's room and hold him prisoner.

Edward's mother, Queen Isabella, had woken up by this stage and desperately tried to get into the room, crying out, 'Fair son, fair son, have pity on gentle Mortimer!' But she was then scared off by armed men marching through the castle and she fled. She was eventually discovered at dawn, in a state of

Nottingham Castle istock

shock. Mortimer was held prisoner in a small space below the castle grounds before being tried before a jury. He was put to death by hanging but his lover was spared from execution and kept under house arrest. After her death her ghost was seen wandering the grounds of the castle in a nightdress. Some have heard screams and cries in Norman French of 'Fair son, have pity on gentle Mortimer'. In the passage below the ground where Mortimer was held prisoner by Edward, now called 'Mortimer's Hole', people have heard footsteps when no one else is there.

Mortimer's Hole istock

Newark Castle

Like Nottingham Castle, the ghosts of Newark Castle are very much associated with politics and power. Visit Newark Castle today and you'll find only the remaining walls of the actual castle and four rooms. Yet, despite this, stories have lingered about ghostly goings-on at the site for many years. The ruins of Newark Castle not only look atmospheric. They have also been the reported site of some very strange experiences.

One of the castle's remaining rooms has a particularly sad association. It was the room in which King John died and it was also said to be the setting for the suicide by hanging of one of the castle rangers in the 1900s. Since then, a number of tour guides have been horrified to walk into the room and

Newark Castle istock

see the apparition of a body hanging and moving around as if it was struggling for breath. If that wasn't enough, people visiting the dungeon have heard the sound of hushed voices at night as well as loud chanting and bangs! But the experiences in the castle dungeons grow even stranger than that. Some people have reported seeing coins or stones being thrown! Visitors have also noticed flashes of light in the castle grounds and have heard screams and shouts coming from the castle wall next to the river.

CITY CENTRE SPECTRES

Today, the National Justice Museum (previously known as the Galleries of Justice) is a hugely popular attraction in Nottingham's Lace Market, voted England's Small Visitor Attraction of the Year in 2014. Being based in the city of Nottingham's old courthouse and jail, you would expect it to have more than its fair share of ghosts. It does. So much so that the National Justice Museum has been voted one of the most haunted buildings in the UK, with the most active poltergeist in the UK! No wonder that the museum is frequently visited by paranormal groups. It has also been featured on television's *Ghost Hunters International* and *Most Haunted*.

The National Justice Museum
Courtesy of Bernard Beilby and www.picturethepast.org.uk

So what are the ghostly presences which make the National Justice Museum such a source of otherworldly activity? They are closely connected with the building's incredible and often disturbing history. The site on which it stands has been associated with crime and punishment since the Saxon times. The first written record of the site being used as a law court goes all the way back to 1375 and it was referred to as a prison for the first time in 1449. Visit the museum today and you get an overwhelming sense of the human suffering which went on there over the years.

This is a complex and historic building which seems to play host to ghosts in all kinds of nooks and crannies. The entrance to the museum alone is said to be inhabited by no fewer than four ghosts! Look out for a lady in a long gown, a man in Victorian clothes and a soldier. The fourth phantom is a little girl who is said to be the cause of cold spots experienced by visitors. She has also been seen on the stairs and in the Grand Jury room. Watch out for the medieval cave where the museum's poltergeist has been experienced, as well as dark shadows and strange sounds.

The dramatic courtroom has been the scene of a great deal of otherworldly phenomena over the years, with visitors hearing footsteps, knocking sounds and groaning. Unexplained noises have also been heard in many other parts of the museum, such as the cells and the corridor leading to the cells, the laundry room, the exercise yard and the 'chapel'. People have also experienced being touched and pushed and finding odd orbs in their photographs. In 2015, a visitor was shocked to notice

The Queen's Medical Centre

Queen's Medical Centre
Courtesy of Lee Haywood

a mysterious figure in a photo that he had taken in one of the museum's cells. The photograph appears to show the ghost of a condemned criminal, with a hangman's hood! If you'd like to experience the museum's strange phenomena for yourself, it regularly hosts ghost tours and other paranormal events!

Just beyond Nottingham city centre, in the leafy area of Wollaton, stands Queen's Medical Centre (or QMC as it's called by locals). Opened in 1977, until 2012 Queen's Medical Centre was the largest hospital in the UK and the largest teaching hospital in Europe. The hospital has had its own share of ghostly tales since the 1970s. Some people say that they have seen a weird apparition in a grey robe walking around the corridors at night. However, it is nowhere to be seen when they look for it! Another story goes that nurses having a quick nap in one of the rest rooms are shaken gently awake by a nurse who tells them it's time to get up. Yet there is no one matching her description working at the hospital!

The Round House

Today, the Round House is a pub in Nottingham city centre. It takes its name, as you might guess, from its distinctively curved shape. However, not so long ago it was the Jubilee Wing of the old Nottingham General Hospital. This is perhaps the reason that the place has been the site of a number of supernatural experiences. Staff at the pub have witnessed figures walking through the bar, then suddenly disappearing into a wall!

The Caves of Nottingham

Nottingham is known for its complex and historic network of sandstone man-made caves lying under the city and further afield. One part of this network is believed to be haunted. Visitors to the City of Caves, an attraction based in the Broadmarsh Shopping Centre, have seen some strange things, like dark shadowy entities visible just on the edge of their vision!

Hopkinson 21

Nottingham city centre boasts plenty of vintage shops and one of its best known is Hopkinson 21 on Station Street. The large shop gained notoriety after reports that the ghost of a former shopkeeper had been seen in the building. CCTV captured a moment in which a strange figure can be seen moving towards a rack of clothes before pausing beside items of clothing. It then turns and moves away, as if floating…

The building is full of history as it was originally opened in the 1880s as a family-run store called H. Hopkinson Ltd. Some believe that the ghost is the wife of the original owner of the shop. Such was the impact of this 'sighting' that it was featured in the national press. You can view the video for yourself by checking the sources link at the end this book. It does look spookily like a ghostly figure has been captured on CCTV!

Trent Bridge

The picturesque bridge that leads to the famous cricket ground is associated with some long-standing ghost stories. People walking or driving over the bridge have seen a dark figure jumping into the river, but when they rush to look into the water, they can't see anything there. Others have seen a figure standing on the bridge staring into the water before disappearing. Some reports describe him as wearing a green jacket. "This is believed to be the ghost of a man who committed suicide by jumping from the bridge many years ago." There have also been other odd sightings of a phantom jogger running over the bridge. He appears to be an everyday jogger, but then he simply disappears.

Trent Bridge istock

British Transport Police Station

Just off to the side of Nottingham Railway Station, you'll find the British Transport Police Station. Bizarrely, its toilets are reported to be haunted! "The story goes that in 1977, an officer working in the building alone one night was startled to hear a door slamming shut." He set off to discover the cause of the noise and found a series of wet footsteps leading to the toilets. But when he followed the trail, he found no one was in the room! Since then, it has been thought that the toilets are haunted by a male ghost. This was backed up by another encounter, many years later, in 2007. In this one, another officer saw a man walk into the toilets. When he went in himself, he couldn't see anyone there.

HAUNTED HALLS
Annesley Hall

Annesley Hall was once a resplendent country house near Mansfield. Sadly, at the time of writing, the Grade II-listed building stands in a serious state of disrepair. It seems that its rich history and its name as one of Nottinghamshire's haunted locations has not protected it from neglect and the damage caused by a major fire a few years ago. Fortunately, there is some progress with a recent application being made to repair the roof.

But the fragile state of the building belies its rich history. It was the ancestral home of the Chaworth-Musters family and back in its heyday, it was inhabited by the Chaworths, distant relatives of the Byrons of Newstead Abbey. There was some shared history with Lord Byron himself, as the young poet fell in love with Mary, the daughter of the house. While this romance came to nothing, we will hear more of Mary later on in this book. Meanwhile, the squire of the house was behaving in a rather Byronesque way himself and got one of the servant girls pregnant. He sent the girl off to stay with an aunt in Northumberland and made regular payments to support her.

Nature took its course and the squire was pleased to receive regular updates on his baby's progress. But one evening, back at Annesley Hall, the servant girl was seen by one of the other servants. She looked ill and strange and ignored people when they called her name. This continued over several weeks and it soon became clear that what people were seeing was a phantom rather than a real-life person. Yet the letters and updates continued from the girl's aunt in Northumberland as if everything was fine. The squire sent a servant to Northumberland to investigate and soon discovered the sad news – the girl had died around the time that her phantom was first seen. The poor little boy had been sent to a workhouse by his greedy aunt, who was keeping the maintenance money for herself. Thankfully, the boy was taken away from the workhouse and sent to live with kinder relatives. The ghost clearly wanted to make sure that something was done to help her child. But she didn't stop after the rescue of her son. She continues to be seen close to the hall in a bonnet and shawl.

The troubled servant girl is not the only ghostly inhabitant of Annesley Hall. The ghost of another woman has been seen there – a woman with long, dark hair which she likes to brush as she sits next to the well in the grounds. There are other weird tales about the hall too, like laughter being heard in the empty stable, the sounds of sudden music, the inexplicable aroma of cigar smoke and the appearance of a strange black dog. Some have seen a peculiar figure staring from one of the windows in the mews. It is thought that this is the ghost of another young servant girl who hanged herself from the staircase in the laundry centuries ago. The ghost of a pregnant woman, rumoured to have been murdered, is also occasionally glimpsed beside a fireplace, holding a baby. In 2010, a group of film-makers making a psychological thriller were unnerved by a series of minor but inexplicable events taking place during their time there. No wonder Annesley Hall has been featured on *Most Haunted*.

You don't have to go far from the hall to find even more ghostly associations. Walk over to the remains of Annesley Old Church next door and you'll be on the spot of sightings of a spectral man wearing a dark cloak. Known locally as the Black Monk of Annesley, his origins are a mystery because there were no monasteries in the area. As with many ghosts, there are a number of theories about this mysterious figure. Some are based on the fact that victims of the bubonic plague are buried on the spot where he is seen. Or is he the spirit of a long-dead vicar? One thing is for sure: Annesley Hall and Annesley Old Church will continue to fascinate ghost-hunters for many years to come.

Bestwood Lodge

Bestwood Lodge was formerly, as the name suggests, a Victorian hunting lodge. Just a few miles from Nottingham city centre, the park it stands in and the area around it was a hunting area of around 3,711 acres. It was part of medieval Sherwood Forest. The enclosed park remained in Crown possession until the 17th century. At this point, King Charles II gave it to his mistress, Nell Gwynn, and their love child, who became the 1st Duke of St. Albans. It was Nell and her son who transformed the lodge into their sanctuary from city life.

These days Bestwood Lodge is a hotel, but the stories of its ghostly inhabitants help to keep its history alive. It is thought that the apparition seen walking in the grounds in 17th-century clothes is the ghost of Nell Gwynn herself! This is a happy ghost. She is said to talk and laugh as if in unseen company.

Bestwood Lodge has been the scene of other otherworldly sightings. In the family room, when children stay, a strange aroma of oranges is smelled. Yet no orange peel is ever found and the smell is only ever noticed when children stay in the room. Hotel guests have also experienced odd things, like locked doors being found open on the guest's return to the room and an overall sense of unease. Hotel staff have also seen shadowy figures walking around, some in old-fashioned clothing.

Bestwood Lodge
Courtesy of Bernard Beilby and www.picturethepast.org.uk

Bunny Hall

Bunny Hall is a Grade I listed country house in the village of Bunny. The Elizabethan red-brick house with its 80-foot-high tower has a rich history. Restored by its owner, the eccentric Sir Thomas Parkyns – known as the 'wrestling baron' – it was later left in a state of neglect before being purchased by a local millionaire. To this day, the ghostly figure of Sir Thomas is seen walking around Bunny in a long coat with gold buttons.

He's not the only spooky visitor around these parts. People have also seen the spirit of a former gardener up at the hall as well as a friendly old couple who just happen to be ghosts. The millionaire who lived at the hall had some strange experiences while living there, so much so that he called in a medium who claimed to have detected 14 otherworldly guests including seven children, a nanny, a groom, a cook and an inebriated butler!

Clifton Hall

Clifton Hall, or the Manor of Clifton, is an imposing-looking manor house located on the bank of the River Trent in the village of Clifton. The Grade I listed building gained notoriety in 2008 because of press reports that its millionaire owner, Anwar Rashid, and his family had left the house because they believed it was haunted by evil spirits! Mr Rashid said that he and his family had had to leave after they heard blood-curdling screams in the corridors late at night, as well as seeing strange figures in the bedrooms and noticing inexplicable blood spots appearing on his baby's clothes! The couple also saw mysterious figures that took the form of their children, like doppelgängers. Apparently, Mr Rashid had been warned about the ghosts of Clifton Hall before he bought the place, but he didn't listen…

The ghost stories about Clifton Hall go back a long way. This isn't surprising, considering that it has been in existence since at least the 11th century. In the 13th century, ownership of the hall was transferred to the Clifton family, the Lords of the Manor of Clifton. It is the period in which the hall was used as the base for Clifton Hall Girls' Grammar School that many of the creepy tales come from. It is said that the sound of a baby crying was heard from a sealed-off room with a bricked-up doorway. The story goes that a maid was jilted by the squire and, in revenge, had grabbed the baby and jumped from the third-floor window, killing herself and the child. People also reported seeing doppelgängers of school students.

Another odd tale associated with Clifton Hall is linked to the River Trent, which connects with the hall via an inlet. It is said that a huge fish-like creature swims upstream to the hall and stays and splashes about in the inlet for three days to foretell the impending doom of the owners of the house!

Colwick Hall
Colwick Hall is a handsome building on an estate with a history which goes back as far as 1362. Now a hotel, the hall is associated with the Byrons, the family of the famous poet, who were based there for many years before they moved to Newstead Abbey, which we'll look at later in this book.

After the Byrons moved on, the Musters family (Jack Musters and his wife Mary Chaworth-Musters) took on the ownership of the hall. They had been living at Annesley Hall, which we looked at earlier on. Now, the ironic thing about this was that Lady Mary had been the childhood sweetheart and some say the only true love of Lord Byron. Despite her association with the poet-to-be, she chose to marry Jack Musters. While Jack and Mary lived their comfortable lives in the handsome hall, everyday life for ordinary Nottinghamshire folk was becoming harder and harder. The tensions between the Musters and the local people were driven by Jack using mantraps and spring guns on the land and also by the Black Act of 1723, which created more than 200 hanging offences for poachers.

When the Reform Bill was thrown out of the House of Lords in 1831, rioters in Nottingham moved from the castle to the hall. They violently made their way in, attacking pictures and furniture. Mary hid in the ballroom with her daughter and friend and then, when the rioters set fire to the hall, they hid in the garden before spending the night in the stables. Understandably, the night of violence had a serious impact on Mary and she died soon afterwards of rheumatic fever. Many believe that the ghost of a woman that has been seen in the hall and grounds is that of Mary. Others argue that it is the ghost of Mary's mother-in-law, while some think that it is the spirit of Mary's friend, who hid with her on that fateful night. Whoever it is, there have been many sightings. The ghost is also said to have been captured in a photograph of a wraith-like figure moving along the east wing. Staff believe that the attics at the hall are particularly haunted.

Wollaton Hall and Park
Courtesy of Lee Haywood

Wollaton Hall

Wollaton Hall, along with its beautiful park, is a place that Nottingham's residents love to visit to walk, explore and enjoy the views. The park plays host to all kinds of events celebrating everything from cars to live music while the hall is now a natural history museum with an impressive collection of stuffed animals. It is also famed for being featured as Wayne Manor in the Batman film *The Dark Knight Rises*! Yet this handsome Elizabethan park and mansion also comes with some ghostly tales of its own.

Probably the hall's most well-known ghoul is that of Lady Middleton in Room 19. These days, you will find Room 19 showcasing an impressive fossil collection. But the story goes that when the hall was still privately owned, that particular room was Lady Middleton's bedroom. Sadly, she had a terrible accident, falling down the stairs and breaking her back, leaving her paralysed from the waist down.

She then took to her bedroom and rarely left it after that. Since her death, her ghost has been seen staring wistfully from the window and walking through the chamber. As well as the ghost of Lady Middleton, a mysterious light, like that of a candle, has been seen through the window of one of the rooms at the hall.

While these odd sightings seem fairly fitting for a beautiful old building like Wollaton Hall, another story about Wollaton Park is somewhat odder. One evening in the 1970s, a group of children visiting the park said that they had seen green, gnome-like men driving around in little cars which moved silently! They reported that there were about 60 of them and that they were wearing Noddy-style caps! The children also said that they saw the men running up into the trees. Was this an encounter with the Little People or ghosts, or just a group delusion? We'll probably never know, but it certainly is one of the strangest stories about otherworldly sightings in Nottinghamshire.

Deer in Wollaton Park
Courtesy of Lee Haywood

MILITARY GHOULS
East Stoke

If you visit East Stoke today, you'll find a small and peaceful village about half a mile east of the River Trent. But its quiet appearance belies its dramatic role in our country's past. The place was actually the scene of what is believed to be the bloodiest battle in British history. This was the Battle of Stoke Field in 1487, which was fought between Yorkist rebels and the army of Henry VII. The Yorkists were beaten by Henry, with many being killed as they retreated to the River Trent; several thousand men died in under three hours. This ended the long civil war known as the Wars of the Roses that had raged for many years.

The site of the Battle of Stoke Field

To this day in Burham Furlong you can see a stone which marks the spot where Henry put up his standard. But there is also said to be another, stranger, memorial of the Battle of Stoke Field – the figure of a man wearing what looks like a helmet and carrying a spear or pike. Other sightings include the figures of naked or part-naked men. Could these be the ghosts of mercenaries captured, stripped and humiliated, as Richard McKenzie suggests in his book, They Still Serve?

The local church also has its own strange story. East Stoke Church is home to a dramatic memorial featuring a large angel. This angel has been seen to shed tears, even on dry days…

RAF Syerston

RAF Syerston, a Royal Air Force station in the parish of Flintham, near Newark, has a long and proud history. It was a bomber base during the Second World War and continues to be used to this day as a base for the Royal Air Force Central Gliding School and the 644 Volunteer Gliding Squadron. A hangar on the site is reputed to have a very strange atmosphere, especially at night. All manner of odd things have taken place in the 'haunted hangar', such as lights turning themselves on and off through the night, even when the place was securely locked up. Even the police dogs at the base have reacted to the atmosphere at RAF Syerston, acting as if they want to get away from the hangar as quickly as possible. There have also been reports of sudden and inexplicable sudden drops in temperature, a classic sign of a paranormal presence.

RAF Syerston

RAF Winthorpe

If you visit the site of RAF Winthorpe, near Newark, today you'll find a popular air museum and various thriving businesses based there. But this place, located near the Lincoln Road, used to serve an important military purpose. RAF Station Winthorpe, No. 51 Base, was opened as a satellite station for RAF Swinderby. The airfield soon grew from its basic beginnings with other squadrons moving in. These teams flew the impressive Stirling and Lancaster bombers. One of these, a Lancaster, was on its way home after being damaged by a German warplane. But despite its fairly stable condition, the plane all at once moved over to the right and landed in the Fleet Stream, leaving no survivors. It is thought that a figure seen in Langford Lane in a blue air force uniform is the ghost of one of the men who died in the crash.

Langford Lane Near Winthorpe

RAF Newton

Today, RAF Newton stands quiet and atmospheric. This former RAF station was used as a bomber base to allow squadrons to re-equip themselves after the Battle of France. It was then used as a flying training school during the Second World War, a role which continued right up to 2000.

This eerie place has been the location of a number of spectral sightings. One of these was the ghost of an airman wandering around close to houses on the site of the old runway. Drivers have stopped to offer the man a lift, but then are shocked to find that he has disappeared! The airbase was even said to have been haunted while it was still operational. Some said that they saw the figure of a Polish airman in the aircrew's mess. Perhaps this was one of the men from the Polish Air Force squadrons housed at the base?

More recently, eerie things have been experienced by catering staff working upstairs, like the feeling of being watched and hearing strange sounds. One of them reported seeing a man in a flying suit and lifejacket move across the room and disappear into a wall. As recently as 2009, a film crew captured what they believed to be ghostly sounds at the airbase. They overheard piano music while they were making their film. During an interview for a documentary about the film, the audio picked up weird and inexplicable swing music in the background.

PUB PHANTOMS
The Admiral Rodney, Calverton

As we will see later in this book, Calverton is packed full of ghosts, if all the stories are to be believed. The Admiral Rodney is said by some to be the most haunted spot in this highly haunted place. This well-established pub is home to more than the usual kind of spirits. It has its own ghost, known as Sarah. While you are unlikely to actually see Sarah, you may feel her presence. Sarah doesn't like to go upstairs and is sensed most often in the pub cellar. One theory is that Sarah is somehow linked to the rumoured underground passage

The Admiral Rodney, Calverton
Courtesy of F.W. Stevenson and www.picturethepast.org.uk

which used to run between the cellar and the vicarage. Years ago, the vicarage was pulled down and this tunnel was blocked off. Some say that perhaps Sarah was a special friend of the vicar's, but we'll probably never know the truth. Whatever her history, Sarah likes to have fun, as the stories of her toying with the pub drinks equipment suggest! According to Rupert Matthews in his book *Haunted Places of Nottinghamshire*, back in 2004 the pub landlord actually walked into the cellar and saw one of the beer taps turning round by itself!

Sarah is not the only ghost to grace the Admiral Rodney. Matthews also recounts tales about a mysterious man in a 1940s or 1950s black suit. He has been seen to walk through the back of the pub and has quite a penchant for slamming doors, even when the door is locked! But there are even more ghostly goings-on at this Calverton pub. Matthews also shares the tale of an elderly gentleman in black who has been seen sitting in the corner having a quiet pint. He is believed to be a regular who obviously felt so at home at the pub that he keeps coming back, even after his death.

The Bell Inn is as packed with history as it is with beer. This old pub dates all the way back to 1437. There is an ongoing local controversy about whether The Bell or one of its two rivals, Ye Olde Trip to Jerusalem and Ye Olde Salutation Inn, is the oldest pub in the city. The history of The Bell goes all the way back to 1276, when Carmelite friars established a friary on the area that is now Friar Lane with land that included a guesthouse on the site of what is now The Bell Inn.

Perhaps it's no surprise that The Bell has its fair share of long-running ghostly tales.

The Bell was owned by the Jackson family for over a hundred years. It seems that one old landlord, Robert Jackson, is

The Bell Inn, Nottingham
Courtesy of Bernard and Pauline Heathcote Photographic Collection and
www.picturethepast.org.uk

unwilling to give up taking care of the pub because his spirit has been seen walking through its restaurant. In *The Ghost Tour of Great Britain: Nottinghamshire* Richard Felix tells the tale of a barmaid who was standing on a ladder when she felt an odd sensation, the feeling that someone or something was behind her... When she looked up, she caught sight of Robert Jackson's ghost disappearing through the wall!

But, as the book also recounts, this is not the only ghost to frequent The Bell. The previous landlord also told the author that one night, after closing time, he heard voices which sounded like those of his grandfather's mother and older brother arguing in one of the downstairs rooms. He went downstairs to investigate, but by the time he got there they had stopped. But when he went back upstairs and unlocked his office door to do some work, he found that the pictures and the calendar on his wall were moving, as if someone was brushing past them! He also felt something brush against his back.

The book also shares the story of a repeated sighting that took place in the pub restaurant in which two men in Edwardian dress appeared and sat down as if waiting for service, before disappearing! It also said that the ladies' toilets are inhabited by a female ghost. Yet another spooky story associated with The Bell is that the ghost of a jester in medieval dress parades around playfully on the pavement in front of it.

Three pubs in Nottingham lay claim to being the city's oldest and all three of them are associated with some creepy ghost

Ye Olde Salutation Inn, Nottingham
Courtesy of K Gardiner and www.picturethepast.org.uk

stories. **Ye Olde Salutation Inn** is one of these. Like its rivals, The Bell Inn and **Ye Olde Trip to Jerusalem**, the Salutation has a long history. Known affectionately by its regulars as the 'Sal', the pub has a name as a rock pub. But while you may often find the place heaving with loud music, it is also visited by some other more unearthly beings, if the stories are to be believed.

Like many places in Nottingham city centre, the Sal is based above a honeycomb of sandstone caves. It is these caves that are the basis for many of the spooky sightings. People have experienced an inexplicable chill and feelings of something touching them, and weird orbs have appeared in photos taken in the pub. The pub is said to be frequented by a figure of street urchin who carries a bunch of roses, who is known affectionately as Rosie. There are also tales of John, the old pub landlord, who is said to show that he has returned to the pub by making the lights in the cellar flicker.

While some say that there is still doubt over which pub can claim even to be the oldest in Nottingham, Ye Olde Trip to Jerusalem confidently claims that it is 'the oldest inn in England'. Whether you agree or not with that statement, there is no denying that the 'Trip', as locals call it, is one of the best-known pubs in Nottingham, thanks to a weird story about a cursed galleon. While it is not strictly a ghost story, the story of the small wooden model of a galleon which used to hang upstairs in the pub is a spooky one. It is said that all the people who have cleaned it have died mysteriously and unexpectedly.

Ye Olde Trip to Jerusalem istock

Some say it is because a former landlord put a curse on it. Successive generations of landlords banned everyone from touching it and years of cobwebs and grime built up on the model. Sadly, it has now been placed in a glass case. I remember seeing the ship when it was suspended from the ceiling in the pub's main upstairs room. There was certainly something eerie about the sight of the little galleon draped in years and years of cobwebs.

While we're on the subject of peculiar tales that aren't quite ghost stories, there is another object at the Trip which is claimed to have special powers, but of quite a different kind. A lovely old antique chair which has stood in the pub's upstairs lounge for years is said to increase a woman's chance of becoming pregnant if she sits on it! The pub website says that the high demand for these special powers means that the chair is now on display only and not for general use!

As well as its objects of curiosity, the Trip also has a reputation for ghostly visitors. Its cellar is based down in the sandstone caves at the foot of Nottingham Castle and is said to be inhabited by a spectre that makes loud banging noises as if it is wearing heavy shoes. In his book *Nottinghamshire Ghosts and Legends*, David Haslam shares the experiences of a former pub landlord and landlady. According to them, the pub's Rock Lounge was the focus of activity, with objects mysteriously disappearing and then reappearing in strange places, and bottles and glasses flying off the shelves. In the book, Haslam tells how staff heard the sound of breaking glass, but found absolutely no sign of damage. He was told by the old landlord and landlady that the pub was haunted when they first started there, and they recounted the story they'd heard of a group of tourists visiting the cellars and seeing a pair of foot soldiers walk through a wall!

The Saracen's Head, Southwell

The Saracen's Head Hotel and Restaurant is just two minutes' walk from Southwell's beautiful minster. The building is packed full of history, having gained constitutional status in 1396. It has been patronised by many illustrious figures, including monarchs, the poet Byron and the writer Dickens. In August 1642, King Charles stayed at the inn en route to Nottingham where he put up the Royal Standard to signal the start of the Civil War. Sadly, Charles was to spend his last night alive at the inn four years later when he was caught and executed by the Roundheads. The inn was eventually taken over by new owners who, not being Royalists, changed the name from the King's Arms to the Saracen's Head. This new name was a direct insult to the Royalists because the King was beheaded by a Saracen sword.

Not long after the name change, the ghost of the dead King began to be seen at the inn. If you stay in the hotel's King Charles Suite today, you are most likely to see him there, for that is where he is most often spotted. However, the monarch's spirit can also be seen in the passageway leading up to the rooms. By all reports, this is a sad ghost who carries the weight of the world on his shoulders and is dressed in dirty clothes.

The Saracen's Head, Southwell David Hallam Jones

But, as if to balance the ghost of the sad king, the Saracen's Head is also inhabited by the spirit of a happy woman. Seen dressed in the costume of the 18th century, this jolly ghost laughs and smiles. Due to changes in the layout, the area that the ghost frequents is now a ladies' toilet, but rather than being startling, even in this setting her friendly outlook has meant that her appearance has been seen as benign.

In his book, *Haunted Places of Nottinghamshire*, Rupert Matthews tells of the 'plate of evil' in the pub restaurant. This was a humble willow pattern plate that hung on one of the restaurant walls. It sounds very normal, apart from the fact that it was hung upside down! As Matthews recounts, the reason for this was that it had been in place since the time of the Great War and locals referred to it as the 'plate of evil', believing in rumours that bad luck would befall anyone who moved it. As the story goes in Matthews's book, new owners who were not from Southwell ordered that the plate be removed as part of their refurbishment plans. But because none of the local workmen would touch it, one of the owners moved it. The tale goes that the owners ran into serious financial difficulties within a matter of weeks and had to sell up. So, was this simply a sign of challenging economic times or was the evil plate taking its revenge?

HAUNTED CHURCHES, ABBEYS AND PRIORIES
St John the Evangelist's Church, Carlton in Lindrick

Walk around Carlton in Lindrick and you can't miss its impressive church with its Saxon stonework and Saxon windows in the tower. Dating from the 7th century, the church is said to be one of the oldest religious foundations in the county. Outside the church door you can see a large stone with a hole in the middle. This imposing sight, which is believed to be no less than 2,000 years old, is known as the 'Devil Stone'. It is the focus of many weird stories. One theory is that the stone is an old font. This could be part of the reason for the belief that ill fortune will befall those who attempt to put it to a use that is not religious. Another theory is that the stone was used for pagan sacrifices using the blood of a virgin. This is thought to be the reason that the ghost of a young girl has been seen near the stone. One local legend says that if you run around the Devil Stone seven times, you may have good luck – or you may meet the devil!

One story about the Devil Stone says that many years ago the stone would be moved into the church each night. Yet somehow it reappeared in its usual spot outside the church without anyone having moved it! The poor locals were fed up as well as being unnerved, so they buried the stone in the graveyard, thinking that this would be the last they would see of it. However, it was then mysteriously dug up again and it is since then that the sightings of the ghost of the young girl have occurred.

St John the Evangelist's Church, Carlton in Lindrick
Courtesy of Mr Philip Robinson and www.picturethepast.org.uk

St Mary's Church in Edwinstowe is well known for its associations with Robin Hood, as it is thought to be the place where Robin and Maid Marion were married! The church is said to be haunted by a number of ghosts, one of which is a green man that some say is the spirit of Robin Hood. St Mary's is also said to be the haunt of a ghostly white nun.

St Mary's, Edwinstowe
Courtesy of Nottinghamshire County Council and www.picturethepast.org.uk

Newstead Abbey Courtesy of Lee Haywood

Newstead Abbey is one of the loveliest places to visit in Nottinghamshire. This handsome old pile in beautiful grounds is forever associated with the poet Lord Byron, being his ancestral home. But its history goes back much further even than Byron's adventures and perhaps that's why it is said to be a spot for some ghostly phenomena.

Despite its name, Newstead has never been an abbey. It was an Augustinian priory which was converted into a domestic home following the Dissolution of the Monasteries. A few years ago I had the opportunity to meet and talk with some of the staff at Newstead Abbey for a community radio project I was involved with. They told us of several unnerving experiences they had had while at work.

Newstead Abbey Courtesy of Lee Haywood

There are many spooky tales told about the odd things seen at the Abbey. Perhaps its most famous ghost is the White Lady. This particular ghost story relates directly to Byron. It starts at the time when Byron decided to leave his beloved Newstead Abbey and sell it to a friend. A woman who was a devoted aficionado of Byron moved into a farmhouse nearby. "Sophie Hyatt was deaf and unable to speak and avoided contact with strangers." However, when the new residents learned about her love for Byron, they encouraged her to visit the Abbey and even to take Byron's old dog (who had stayed behind) for walks. Dressed in her customary light-coloured clothing, Sophie gained the name locally of the 'Little White Lady of Newstead'.

Sadly, the family income supporting her ended so she decided to go to America to try to contact another relative and ask for their help. After leaving a note for the Wildman family telling them what she was doing, she started on her journey to Nottingham to catch the stagecoach to London. As soon as the family found the note, Mr Wildman set off quickly in order to offer Sophie somewhere to stay in the grounds of Newstead for life. The rider and horse raced off to Nottingham but when they reached Nottingham's Old Market Square, they discovered a crowd around a horse and cart next to a pub. It was Sophie, who was dead. She had tragically been run over by the wagon, her deafness preventing her from hearing the driver's warning. But Sophie's days of delight wandering around Byron's old home were not over. Her ghost has been seen in the beautiful gardens, particularly on one path, now known as White Lady's Walk.

Another ghostly tale of Newstead Abbey goes thus... Back in the 1930s, a woman living in Newstead village was close to giving birth. Her husband called the local doctor to get to their house as soon as possible. The doctor was delayed and was only just in time to help with the birth. The husband asked what had caused him to be so late. The doctor told him that he would have been even later if it hadn't been for a monk in black robes who was standing by a waterfall in the grounds of the abbey. The doctor had asked him the way to the village. The monk did not utter a word, but pointed in the direction of the village. The doctor was very unnerved when told that there had been no monks at the abbey for many hundreds of years!

iStock

But the Black Friar or Black Monk, as he is known, is not the only ghostly religious figure to have been seen at the Abbey. There are also rumours of another kind, this time based on a story about Byron himself. A creepy figure called the Goblin Friar was said to appear in front of the head of the Byron family before something bad happened to someone in the family. Byron saw the friar just before his marriage to Anne Milbanke. The disastrous marriage lasted only a year. Lord Byron also told of his experience of seeing a strange column of white vapour rising from the floor. It vanished without a trace while he looked at it.

Two other well-known ghost stories of Newstead Abbey relate to past residents. Sir John Byron lived there in the 17th century. He was known as 'Little Sir John with the Great Beard'. Sadly, the man died just a few hours after his wife. Not long after these tragic events, servants refused to set foot into the library because they said they could see Sir John seated in his usual spot in front of the fire, relaxing while smoking a pipe and reading a book! However, this apparition did not stay long, disappearing forever after six months.

Another story tells of one of the Abbey's owners hearing the sound of a roller being dragged over the gravel in the grounds in the middle of the night. His gardener said that it wasn't his doing. But somehow the estate's huge roller had been moved and padlocked to the side of a gatepost. Was this just a prank or was there something more sinister at work?

Another odd sighting at the Abbey is that of the ghost called the Cavalier. People have seen smoke or mist rising from the floors. Perhaps it is the same as the weird vapour once spotted by Byron. In one sighting, a member of staff saw smoke pouring out from under a door. Worried about fire, she rushed in, but discovered nothing, until she looked across the room into the large mirror hanging there and saw the reflection of a Cavalier, complete with sword and fancy feathered hat! Yet another unsettling presence at the Abbey is the weird aroma of roses and lavender that people have noticed at the bottom of one particular staircase. This presence is now known as 'the Rose Lady'.

While not strictly a ghost story, one of the traditions around Newstead points to its past. The Abbey is home to a huge number of rooks and they have been treated with respect for many years. This is not only for animal welfare reasons but also because the rooks were thought to be the souls of the 'Black Monks' because they were seen to observe the Sabbath by flying off and returning every day except Sunday. This was so well established that, going against what was sadly common practice in the country, the rooks at Newstead Abbey weren't shot but were left alone.

Could **Rufford Abbey** be one of the most haunted places in England? Many think so. Various stories abound about this country estate. While it started out as a Cistercian abbey, it was turned into a country house in the 16th century. One of the best-known stories of Rufford Abbey was told by the mother of the author Vita Sackville-West, who was staying there with her friends, the Savile family. The woman told of how she had been woken up in the night by a horrible feeling of clamminess, as if she was in contact with cold skin! She was more than a little unnerved to learn that there was a ghost of a child murdered at the abbey many years before. The poor thing liked to climb into bed with people for comfort.

There is even more to tell of unhappy phantoms at Rufford. Another spirit seen there is the figure known as the White Lady. She has been seen flickering and moving around the ruins of the Abbey. She is said to be the ghost of Arabella Stuart. Arabella was looking very likely to become queen of England after the death of Elizabeth I, thanks to her royal connections. Instead, she died as a prisoner in the Tower of

Rufford Abbey istock

London. The White Lady has been seen in various parts of the Abbey over the years. As recently as 2013 there were reports in the national press about a photo that was believed to have captured an image of the White Lady.

Yet another story tells of a small elderly lady in black making a ghostly appearance at the Abbey. This tale was told by one of the owners of the house, Lord Savile. He also wrote about the Black Friar of the Abbey and recounted how one of his guests had been visited by 'a gigantic monk with a death's head under his cowl'. According to some early records, one entry actually records that a man died of fright after seeing the Rufford ghost!

Ancient places seem to attract long-standing stories of spirit visitors. No wonder, then, that **Worksop Priory**, dating back to 1103, is the location of a number of spooky sightings. While it is no longer a priory, it is still said to be visited by monks, only in spirit form.

Perhaps one of the best-known ghosts of Worksop Priory is that of a figure which runs along the top of the tower late at night. He has been seen to act in a very excited manner, leaping around and staring over the tower as if he has seen a disturbing sight. No one knows why the ghost monk acts the way he does, but he continues to do so after all these years.

Worksop Priory
Courtesy of Nottingham City Council and www.picturethepast.org.uk

The Priory is also home to another ghost: the Blue Lady. She has been spotted on her way from the gatehouse to the church. Another Priory spirit is more of a sound that a sight: the noise of disembodied footsteps walking heavily on the iron floor grates.

TOWNS WITH GHOSTLY TALES
Mansfield

As Nottinghamshire's largest market town, Mansfield is a busy plae with a rich mining heritage. But it also has its fair share of ghosts, as we will discover.

Theatres seem to attract ghosts. But the apparition said to haunt Mansfield's **Palace Theatre** is a particularly odd one. The observer claimed that they suddenly saw a pair of yellow boots walking across the stage, by themselves. But when she called to someone else to look, the boots stopped and disappeared!

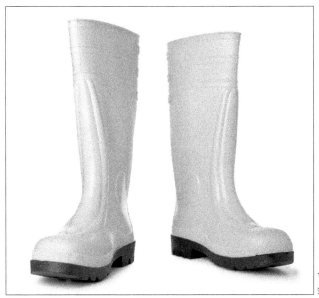

iStock

The Oak Tree is a popular pub on Mansfield's Southwell Road. It is said to take its name from the oak tree which used to stand nearby. Sadly, the history of the tree included a past as a hanging tree, when it was used as gallows. Locals believe that the last person to be hanged from these gallows was a man who had been wrongfully accused. His unquiet spirit has been seen wandering around the area and some even believe they have seen him in the pub. Now affectionately named Timothy, the ghost is described as wearing a dark coat with a high collar. He appears to be upset and has even been heard to say to some observers, 'I did not do it!' before disappearing.

The Village is an old building right in the centre of Mansfield. Now described as a 'party entertainment venue', it was once the biggest nightclub in the town. Before that, back in the 1800s, it was a slaughterhouse and a malthouse. Going even back further than this, a barn stood on the same spot. This was apparently used as a hideout by monks from a nearby church during the time of persecution. The tale goes that, tragically, seven monks died when the barn was set on fire.

Hundreds of years later The Village now has a reputation as a site of interest for paranormal investigators. Its ghosts are said to include a man who is thought to be Mr Merryweather, ex-owner of the malthouse. Another ghostly resident of The Village is the spirit of a woman called Catherine who drowned in the River Maun, which runs beneath the building. Paranormal investigators have noted all kinds of weird occurrences, including a piano playing by itself and the sound of a baby crying. As recently as April 2016 The Village hit the national news because of video footage showing a weird mist seen during a ghost hunt in the building. Some people believe it to be the spirit of those seven poor monks who died tragically so many years before.

Newark

Newark is another of Nottinghamshire's market towns. It has an interesting history with origins that are thought to be Roman. It is most probably this heritage that has led to the town having more than its fair share of ghost stories.

Newark's pubs seem to be popular with ghostly visitors. The picturesque **White Hart Inn** claims to be Newark's oldest pub. Perhaps that is what lies behind the tales of its ghost, a poltergeist who goes by the name of George. He harks back to a more brutal age when criminals could be sentenced to death. While most local criminals would have been taken to Nottingham for punishment, some would be dealt with on their home turf. So it was with George and now it is believed that his spirit haunts the pub to this day. The book *The Great Ghost Tour of Great Britain: Nottinghamshire* tells of author Richard Felix's conversations with a member of staff from the pub who has seen coins suddenly fly across the room when other members of staff were having an argument. Does conflict make the spirit uncomfortable? Another story in the book tells of a clock with hands that used to move without any human intervention! As the book's author comments, these incidents always seem to occur when there is a negative atmosphere in the pub.

It is said that a rather grumpy ghost, the figure of an elderly man, haunts the **Old Kings Arms** in Kirkgate. The ghost has been known to move furniture around, turn lights off and even to slam doors! At Newark's **Woolpack Pub** there are tales of a grey lady who is occasionally spotted in the main bar. **The Bakery Tea Rooms** is a lovely old place which is known for good teas but also for being home to a ghost; this spirit is thought to be that of a little girl.

Newark Cemetery is associated with rumours of the spirit of an airman. Dressed in a blue RAF uniform, he wanders around the tombstones. Newark is haunted by other military figures, too. In Appleton Gate, people have heard the sounds of men preparing to ride horses and then galloping off. Some

Newark Market Place iStock

say that these are the soldiers of Prince Rupert preparing to face the Roundheads.

One particularly weird tale is the one which tells the story of ghostly digging sounds coming from **Newark Market Place**. These peculiar noises are believed to be the spirits of the Scots miners brought in to tunnel into the hill during the final stages of the siege of Newark in 1646.

The building which was once the **Ossington Coffee Palace** is a striking one. It stands in all its finery close to Newark's Castle Station. It was built by Viscountess Ossington in 1882 to provide a place where travellers could stay without being tempted by alcohol, as none was served on the premises. The

The former Ossington Coffee House John Sutton

building was meant to continue in this way after the Viscountess's death but that all changed in the 1960s when it was sold and went on to become a public house. After that, the portrait of Viscountess Ossington which hung in the building was said to 'fly off the wall' several times! Newark and Sherwood District museum service purchased the painting in 1981 and it is now kept safely somewhere else. "However, it is said that there are still signs of a benevolent ghost in the basement to this day."

This avoids both naming the business and suggesting that they gave us a special statement about otherworldly activity in their building! Could it be that the spirit of Viscountess Ossington continues to keep an eye on the building to this day?

Retford

Retford is an old market town with some lovely Georgian buildings and is known for its part in the tale of the Pilgrim Fathers, the people who fled to America in 1620 after being persecuted for their religious beliefs. But Retford has its fair share of ghostly residents too. Let's go first to **The White Hart**, which was, until its closure not that long ago, a handsome Georgian hotel. You can still see the old coach entrance today. The story goes that it is was in this very archway that a girl tragically died when she was hit by a coach going into the stable yard. Since then, the ghost of a girl has been seen in the hotel courtyard. But she is not in distress. She runs around joyfully. It is said that some observers have assumed that she is a real girl dressed in costume and so they are very shocked to see her suddenly vanish!

Touchingly, the hotel had a bust made as a memorial to the girl and this could still be seen in the main room of the hotel up until its recent closure. But it was said that a curse had been placed on the bust by the girl's grieving father. No one was allowed to touch it, let alone remove it from the hotel, to warn drivers to be more careful in the future. However, the story goes that during a refurbishment in the eighties, a workman ignored strict instructions and chipped the statue. Within moments the entire ceiling of the bar collapsed! From then on, a box was placed around the sculpture to protect it from any more accidents.

Not far from the White Hart Hotel is Retford's fine town hall. There have been sightings of a Victorian lawyer on the hall's staircase and in one of the upstairs offices. He is dressed in full wig and gown regalia, but walks by in a state of apparent ease. Over at Retford's **Little Theatre**, people have seen a ghostly man in black and have had experiences of weird cold draughts and the sounds of footsteps when no one else is there.

Head to Retford's North Road and you'll find the very stately **West Retford Hotel**. The sightings here are said to be linked to the building's past as a private home. The lady of the house had an affair with the stable hand and when the news got back to her husband, the stable hand committed suicide. Years later, the ghostly figure of a lady was seen walking around the hotel and into the courtyard which leads to the stables. She is believed to be the ghost of the poor woman. She has even been seen near the reception, and the door has been seen to open and shut without any human help. In Haunted Places of

Nottinghamshire, Rupert Matthews tells the tale of how, in 2004, a maid went up the stairs to clean a room. She saw a woman coming down and stepped aside to allow the guest to pass by, then was shocked to realise that the figure had vanished!

EERIE VILLAGES
Beckingham

Beckingham is a pretty and quiet place. But it too has its ghostly resident, though this one doesn't take a human form! The spot where the Old Trent Road runs from the church to the water meadows is the location of ghostly sightings of an enormous black dog! This terrifying creature is described as being almost as tall as a man, with eyes which seem to glow red from within. Observers have reported seeing the strange dog-like creature walk out from the churchyard, go down the road and then turn off to go across the water meadows.

So what is this peculiar creature and what is its purpose? Some say that it is the spirit of a dog that guarded the local squire many years ago. One story goes that a brave man tried to block the path of the dog and ask it what it was doing. The dog stared at the man, who then fainted and was never himself again after the encounter. Some people believe that the black dog of Beckingham is a version of Black Shuck, a curious canine figure which can either be an omen of death or have a more companionable purpose. A strange ghost dog also makes an appearance in my Ghost Stories of Lincolnshire.

While it is not a big place, the village of **Calverton** is packed full of history. So you would expect it to have its fair share of ghostly tales. And it does!

Calverton
Courtesy of R Iliffe and www.picturethepast.org.uk

One area of Calverton is called **George's Hill** or George's Lane. It is said to be avoided in the dark today by many people – including taxi drivers! This is because of the eerie tales told about a creepy figure in black that haunts the area. The sightings range from a pair of legs running across the road to a shapeless black mass! Some say that the apparition is the ghost of a hitchhiker. Others say that is the unquiet spirit of a man who hanged himself from a tree near the bend on the road. Having spoken to residents of Calverton fairly recently, there seems little doubt that this story is well and truly alive. To this day, drivers have had some seemingly inexplicable experiences when they dare to travel along George's Hill…

Head into the centre of Calverton and you'll soon see an attractive pub, the **Admiral Rodney**, which we have already visited in the chapter on pub phantoms. As well as the other sprits that were described there, it is said to be haunted by one of the old innkeepers, from the 1800s, a man called Tom. His figure has been seen in various parts of the pub. He's not alone. The ghostly figures of children have also been seen. Aside from these, the pub has a resident poltergeist who, over the years, has spotted throwing clothes and kitchen utensils around! This is believed to be the ghost of a servant girl who once worked at the pub.

Calverton also has spectres that like to move around the village. If you go for a walk in the area, watch out for the ghost of a man in a tweed suit and flat cap. He is thought to be the spirit of an old teacher from the village school. There is also the figure of a woman in white, who waits at one of the village bus stops, seemingly forever. There were also tales of odd goings-on at Calverton Hall, which was used as a vicarage. It was knocked down and replaced on the site by the Miner's Welfare and then replaced by a road called Old Hall Close. **Calverton Hall** was the centre of strange sightings, some of which are thought to be of the White Lady mentioned earlier.

Even when the hall was being demolished, weird things happened… One night, the two men doing the demolition work heard the sound of pacing along the floor in one of the rooms, but when they went up to investigate they realised that it was a room from which they had already moved the floorboards! Then they heard a crash followed by silence…

The story goes that soon after this, a discovery was made that one of the maids at the hall had been jilted on her wedding day and committed suicide. Could this sad event be the explanation for the strange activities at the hall?

The story doesn't quite end there. There have been weird sightings on the road where the hall once stood. Drivers have seen a figure of a woman suddenly appear as if from nowhere. But when they swerve, they can't see her any more.

Scrooby is a small Nottinghamshire village with a long-standing ghost story. The tale goes that people travelling along

Scrooby
Courtesy of Nottinghamshire County Council and www.picturethepast.org.uk

71

the Great North Road just beyond the village had to pay to use the road. The money was kept in the toll-keeper's cottage. However, one evening a man called John Spencer broke into the cottage to steal the money. The noise he made woke the toll-keeper and his wife and he ended up killing them both. Spencer was apprehended and was hanged right next to the Great North Road. Since then, the site of the hanging has been haunted by a ghost in the form of a man in a long, black cloak. Some drivers believe he is a hitchhiker, stop to offer him a lift and are startled to see him disappear!

Gunthorpe

Tucked away by the River Trent, the Unicorn Hotel in Gunthorpe looks like a peaceful place. But it is associated with many long-standing ghostly tales. The stories include experiences of the covers being pulled off occupied beds by a ghostly hand. This is said to be the work of the spirit of a small girl who tries to bother guests she doesn't like the look of!

Another spooky story about Gunthorpe is the strange creature which has been seen near the water meadows by the River Trent. As the light fades, observers have been startled to see something that looks like a huge cat, panther or dog. It walks along beside the river and then disappears!

Gunthorpe
Courtesy of Nottingham City Council and www.picturethepast.org.uk

Ruddington

A bakery in Ruddington was the source of spooky stories for a long time. Now converted into flats, the old Horspool bakery was the focus of rumours, particularly in the 1950s and the 1960s. People claimed to have had sightings of a tall man in a blazer and tie. He appeared to be quite real as he walked through the village to the bakery, but would then disappear! Sadly, he has not been spotted for some time. The village is also the centre of stories about a ghostly train seen running along the old railway line to Nottingham, even though the line hasn't been used for years!

WEIRD WOODS
Harlow Wood

If you travel along the A60 about half a mile north from the junction with the B6020 Kirkby Road, opposite Thieves Wood in Harlow Wood, Mansfield, you'll find a humble little memorial stone. It commemorates Elizabeth Shepherd, who was murdered at the age of 17 on 7 July 1817. Poor Elizabeth, or Bessie as she was also known, had set off from her home in Papplewick to find work in Mansfield. The next day, having found work, Bessie was walking back home along the Nottingham Road, past Harlow Wood. She was seen by a man who was sleeping under a hedge and he murdered her. The man, Charles Rotherham, was arrested and was hanged in Nottingham.

The local community was horrified by what had happened to poor Bessie and they organised a collection to raise money for a monument. When the road was widened in the 1930s, the stone was moved slightly and then moved again in the 1960s, with another more permanent inscription being added to the opposite side. However, this is where the story becomes more intriguing, because the legend attached to the stone is that if it is disturbed the ghost of Bessie Shepherd will appear. So, for a few days after it was first moved in the 1930s, Bessie's ghost was seen. The story goes that in the 1950s the stone was hit by a car and again a ghostly apparition was seen nearby.

Another strange tale about the stone goes that in 1988 the headstone of Elizabeth's grave went missing. Two local policemen posed by the memorial stone for a photograph for the local press. One of the men felt compelled to touch the stone and then suddenly had a strong urge to go back to the churchyard, where they found the headstone underneath a hedge and not far from the grave!

The ghost of Bessie Shepherd continues to be seen close to the monument to this day. Startled drivers have been shocked when stopping to offer the woman a lift to see her suddenly disappear. Bessie's ghost was even seen by staff working at the old Harlow Wood Orthopaedic Hospital nearby.

Sherwood Forest and the Major Oak

The Major Oak is an impressive sight in Sherwood Forest and an important remnant of local history, so it seems a fitting place to end our exploration of the ghost stories of Nottinghamshire. The huge tree was said to have provided shelter to Robin Hood and his merry men. Weighing no less than 23 tons, it has a girth of 33 feet (10 metres), a canopy of 92 feet (28 metres) and is up to a thousand years old! But as well as a great deal of history, a strange story is associated with the Major Oak. It is thought that the tree is inhabited by a mysterious ghostly figure. Some say it is a tall man dressed in green while other describe it as a bear-like creature. Whatever form it takes, it leaves people visiting the tree with the feeling that a malevolent force is following them.

Major Oak istock

More Ghost Stories from Bradwell Books for you to enjoy

BLACK COUNTRY & BIRMINGHAM

CAMBRIDGESHIRE

CHESHIRE

CORNISH

COTSWOLDS

CUMBRIAN

DERBYSHIRE

DORSET

ESSEX

GLASGOW

HAMPSHIRE AND THE ISLE OF WIGHT

HEREFORDSHIRE

KENT

LANCASHIRE

LEICESTERSHIRE

LINCOLNSHIRE

LONDON

LONDON UNDERGROUND

NORFOLK

NOTTINGHAMSHIRE

OXFORDSHIRE

SCOTTISH

SHROPSHIRE

SOMERSET

STAFFORDSHIRE

SURREY

www.bradwellbooks.co.uk

www.nottinghampost.com/nottingham-ghostbusters-hang-county-s-spookiest/story-28785424-detail/story.html#1khUAkVWhDU3ZwuX.99

www.nottinghampost.com/ghost-nottingham-shopkeeper-mrs-hopkinson/story-29324904-detail/story.html

www.mirror.co.uk/news/weird-news/ghost-former-shopkeeper-spotted-roaming-8062426

www.huffingtonpost.co.uk/entry/spooky-footage-reveals-spirits-of-7-dead-monks_uk_57160a52e4b0dc55ceeb0116

www.dailymail.co.uk/news/article-3547328/Holy-ghosts-Paranormal-expert-claims-eerie-footage-swirling-mist-coming-spirits-seven-restless-monks.html

www.dailymail.co.uk/news/article-2518153/White-Lady-Rufford-Abbey-ghost-photo-captured-using-iPod-Touch.html

www.bbc.co.uk/nottingham/citylife/ghostsandlegends/triptales_1.shtml

www.nottinghampost.com/haunting-goings-county/story-12271704-detail/story.html#PvPXCjFQstcdyFDs.99

www.triptojerusalem.com/history

www.nottinghampost.com/hallowe-en-10-haunted-spots-nottingham-notts/story-19869216-detail/story.html#aycFfdYzKsFWhoOy.99

www.telegraph.co.uk/news/newstopics/howaboutthat/3042568/Spooked-businessman-flees-haunted-mansion.html

www.nottinghamshire.gov.uk/planning-and-environment/country-parks/bestwood/history-of-bestwood

www.nottinghampost.com/film-makers-spooked-annesley-hall-ghouls/story-12223422-detail/story.html

www.galleriesofjustice.com/galleries_of_justice_hauntings.html
www.dailymail.co.uk/news/article-2786889/Is-eerie-figure-
snapped-medieval-prison-site-ghost-condemned-criminal-
wearing-hangman-s-hood.html
http://www.nottinghampost.com/nottingham-s-galleries-justice-
appear-haunted/story-22910703-
detail/story.html#zmq6qtWZJwrtojmj.99
www.huffingtonpost.co.uk/2014/10/10/ghost-condemned-
criminal-hangmans-hood-photographed-prison-
cell_n_5964418.html
https://hauntedhistoryoflincolnshire.blogs.lincoln.ac.uk/newark-
2/castle/

Wayne Anthony, Haunted Nottingham: Myths,
Magic and Folklore (Breedon Books, 2008)
Richard Felix, The Ghost Tour of Great Britain:
Nottinghamshire (Breedon Books, 2006))
Rupert Matthews, Haunted Places of Nottinghamshire
(Countryside Books, 2005)
Catherine Staton, A Ghostly Guide to Nottinghamshire
(Walk & Write, 2008)